Growing and Using Stevia

The Sweet Leaf from Garden to Table
with 35 Recipes

Jeffrey Goettemoeller
and
Karen Lucke

Prairie Oak Publishing
Maryville, Missouri

Copyright © 2008 by Jeffrey Goettemoeller & Karen Lucke

All Rights Reserved

ISBN 978-0-9786293-3-5

Library of Congress Control Number: 2008925032
Library of Congress Subject Headings:
Stevia rebaudiana
Cookery (Stevia)
Herb gardening

Photos by Jeffrey Goettemoeller

2.0

Prairie Oak Publishing
221 South Saunders St.
Maryville MO 64468
www.PrairieOakPublishing.com
www.GrowingStevia.com

Contents

Figures

Acknowledgements

The authors would like thank their mother, Bertha Goettemoeller. She generously assisted in developing many of the recipes in this book. Thanks also to other family members who helped in many ways, especially as taste testers!

The late Dr. Alex Ching deserves a special expression of gratitude. As a professor of plant science at Northwest Missouri State University, Dr. Ching introduced Jeffrey to Stevia and other fascinating plants. He was always energetic and full of enthusiasm, especially about his faith and about plants that could help farmers and consumers. In 1998, Dr. Ching gave Jeffrey the chance to conduct an undergraduate research project, *Seed germination in Stevia rebaudiana.* A link to study results can be found at www.steviaseed.com.

Introduction

STEVIA, THE SWEET LEAF OF SOUTH AMERICA

The leaves of *Stevia rebaudiana* are much sweeter than common sugar. No wonder it's sometimes called "sweet leaf" in Paraguay and Brazil where it originated. Stevia leaves, though, are low-glycemic, low-calorie,[1] and do not encourage

Fig. 0-1: Branched Stevia sprig.

---

1. A 2004 study confirmed stevia leaf is lower in calories than aspartame, much sweeter than sucrose, and has a lower glycemic index as compared to sucrose: S.M. Savita and others, 2004 "Stevia rebaudiana—A Functional Component for Food Industry," Journal of Human Ecology 15 (4): 261-264.

dental cavities.[2] All this makes stevia a great natural alternative to sugar and artificial sweeteners.

Stevia does not taste exactly like sugar. It has a unique flavor; much like honey or maple syrup have their own flavors—especially in the case of whole green stevia. Most people find the taste pleasant when the proper amount is used to make tea or combined with compatible ingredients.

The Problem with Refined Sugar

Why avoid sugar? It's fine in moderation, but refined sugar adds lots of calories to the diet without contributing significant amounts of nutrients. The average American diet includes so many of these empty calories, there's little room for needed nutrients. This can lead to malnutrition and obesity.

A 2005 Penn State study found the average U.S. preschooler gets 14–17 teaspoons of *added* sugar per day![3] Twelve percent of the 4 and 5 year-olds surveyed got more than 25% of their calories from added sugar. These children also had the lowest consumption of most nutrients. They didn't get enough grains, vegetables, fruits, and other nutrient-rich foods.

Another issue with refined sugar, white flour, and other foods with a high glycemic index is that they enter the blood stream quickly, leading to rapid fluctuations in blood sugar levels. Finally, too much sugar can encourage tooth decay and more time at the dentist's office.

---

2. A University Of Illinois College Of Dentistry study found that neither Stevioside nor Rebaudioside A (the main sweet glycosides in stevia) was cariogenic (promoting of dental cavities) under the conditions of the study: S. A. Das and others. 1992. "Evaluation of the Cariogenic Potential of the Intense Natural Sweeteners Stevioside and Rebaudioside A". *Caries Research*. 26 (5): 363.

3. S. Kranz, H. Smiciklas-Wright, A. M. Siega-Riz, and D. Mitchell. 2005. "Adverse Effect of High Added Sugar Consumption on Dietary Intake in American Preschoolers," *Journal of Pediatrics* 146 (1): 105-111.

What About Artificial Sweeteners?

Concerns have been raised about some artificial sweeteners. Aspartame, for example, has been a major cause of health related complaints to the FDA (U.S. Food and Drug Administration).[4] Stevia, on the other hand, has not prompted reports of health problems despite being used in large quantities since the 1970's in countries such as Japan.[5]

Shopping for Stevia

Stevia products are available at natural food stores and online retailers. Refer to chapter 8 for complete information and conversion rates. Dried or fresh leaves (whole) are great for making herb tea. When dried leaves are powdered, you have Green Stevia Powder, which has a unique flavor. It works well in certain recipes and contains beneficial nutrients such as chromium. Since it can be made from homegrown plants, Green Stevia Powder is the main Stevia product used in this book's recipes.

White Stevia Extract Powder is around 90% glycosides (the main sweet constituents of Stevia). With proper modifications, most recipes work well with Stevia Extract Powder. It has little taste of its own. Look for a product without fillers like maltodextrin. Fillers usually contribute carbohydrates. Besides, the pure Stevia Extract Powder or Green Stevia Powder is a better buy. Jeffrey's book, *Stevia Sweet Recipes: Sugar-Free—Naturally!*, features mainly recipes using Stevia Extract Powder.

---

4. cf. Centers for Disease Control (CDC). 1984. "Evaluation of consumer complaints related to aspartame use". MMWR. *Morbidity and Mortality Weekly Report.* 33 (43): 605-7.

5. cf. Daniel Mowery, Ph.D., *Life with Stevia: How Sweet it is!* 1992. Available online: http://healthfree.com/stevlife.html.

Why Use Stevia?

We encourage people to use Stevia for the reasons anyone switches to artificial sweeteners—to avoid calories and avoid fluctuations in blood sugar levels. But *Stevia rebaudiana* is not at all artificial. Stevia is an herb that has been used for centuries! Most importantly, Stevia has a track record of safety and helps dishes taste great when used correctly.

Fig. 0-3: Stevia leaf.

Fig. 0-2: Stevia plant sprig.

Fig. 0-4:
Stevia blossoms.
Magnified cluster of 5 blossoms.

Chapter 1

ABOUT THE STEVIA PLANT

Plant Description

Stevia rebaudiana is a fascinating plant, native to higher altitudes of Paraguay and Brazil in South America. Stevia is the genus. Rebaudiana is the species. When we say "Stevia" in this book, we are referring to this particular species. Only this species, out of the many found in the Americas, contains the high concentration of sweet glycosides making this "sweet leaf" such a useful and amazing herb.

There seems to be something about Stevia that makes many insects reluctant to dine on the leaves. Perhaps Stevia developed its glycosides as an adaptation to protect itself from insect attack.

Stevia is not a particularly showy plant. Sweet taste is its most notable feature. Leaves are much sweeter than stems. It is a non-woody herb with somewhat stiff and brittle stems. Leaves are narrow and notched on the end and sides, ranging from 1-3 inches (25-76 mm) in length.

Plants started from seed sometimes feature larger leaves than do plants started from cuttings. Plants usually reach a height of around 24–30 inches (61-76 cm) under cultivation. Older plants can send up new shoots from underground.

Stevia blossoms are white, tiny, and so numerous that blooming plants can look like clouds. Stevia is a tender perennial, meaning it survives winters, but only where winters are mild. This would include subtropical regions of North America like Florida, the Gulf coast, and coastal California. Unprotected plants usually do not survive temperature below about 25° F. (−4° Celsius) for an extended period of time.

Day Length

Stevia may be grown as an annual (planted every year) where cold winters prevent perennial production. There are advantages to growing Stevia at higher latitudes, closer to the poles. It has to do with the longer summer days.

Stevia is a "short day" plant. This means it generally blooms as days grow shorter in late summer or fall. In northern Missouri (around 40° north latitude), most Stevia plants don't start blooming until late September—too late for a seed crop. On the positive side, though, plants can grow all summer under long daylight conditions at higher latitudes. Long days have the opposite effect that short days do. They encourage leaf growth rather than blossoms, resulting in higher leaf yields and a higher concentration of sweet glycosides.

Many regions with cold winters, then, are great for summer stevia leaf production. But subtropical regions with mild winters allow for a longer growing season, perennial culture, and outdoor seed production.

Stevia in the Wild

Stevia tends to grow wild near bodies of water, where the soil is moist, but not waterlogged, somewhat sandy, and high in organic matter. Its native range is subtropical.

Wild Stevia seems to spread primarily through natural layering (stems fall and strike root) or tillering (shoots sprout from roots near the crown). Blossoms are produced in profusion and pollinated by wind or insects. The tiny, slender seeds are tan or black. But seeds from wild plants are often not viable.[6]

---

6. cf. Clinton C. Shock. 1982. "Rebaudi's stevia: natural noncaloric sweeteners," California Agriculture, September-October: 4-5.

Chapter 2

Outdoor Soil and Culture

Stevia will grow on most garden soils, but prefers sandy loam or loam, high in organic matter. Stevia generally wants to be treated like other herb or vegetable crops, but is a little more sensitive to drying out on one hand and water-logging on the other. Stevia tolerates a wide range of soil pH. Its native soils are on the acid side.

Keys to growing Stevia include the following:

1. compost/organic matter
2. raised beds for heavy soil
3. consistent soil moisture

Garden Soil

A good way to improve heavy, high clay soil or light, sandy soil is to dig or till in good compost. Various composts and composted manures are available for purchase or you can make your own. In most cases, good compost will be the only fertilizer needed.

Making Compost

Composting can involve shredding, frequent turning, and the use of tumblers, but there is a simpler method if you don't mind a longer wait. Use two bins about 3 feet (1 meter) across and 3 feet high, made from mesh fencing, bricks, plastic, or wood, with holes for ventilation. Place 3–6 inches (8–15 cm) of high-carbon material such as leaves, straw, or old hay in one of the bins as a base. Put your vegetable-derived garbage in the bin each day and cover with some of the high-carbon material.

When the bin is full, use the other bin and let the first one sit a few months, turning occasionally with a digging fork. Water the pile if it doesn't rain for a couple of weeks.

For more compost, layer barnyard manure with the dry material and let sit several months, mixing occassionally. Spread finished compost a couple inches (5–6 cm) deep on your growing beds and dig it in or sift for use in potting soil. Compost can also be used as a top dressing around existing plants.

Building Raised Beds

Before building beds, spread any compost or other fertilizers. Till or spade the garden deeply. The soil should be somewhat dry for this. You should be able to squeeze a handful and have it break when dropped.

Mark bed edges with strings or hoses. About 3–4 feet (1–1.25 meters) is the usual bed width. You should be able to reach the middle. You may want paths wide enough for a garden cart.

Dig soil from paths and toss on beds until they are 3–8 inches (8-20 cm) higher than paths. You can install plastic, wood, or brick sides. This makes it easier to use weed guard fabric in the paths, covered by wood chips, stones, or patio blocks. Wood sides should be untreated. A rot resistant type such as cedar will last longer.

Beds without sides sometimes need re-shaping. Make a flat-topped bed with sloping sides or a low arch gradually sloping to the path.

The idea with raised beds is to walk on paths; never on the beds. The lack of compaction, combined with mulching, compost, and earthworm activity, will eventually create fertile, easily worked soil.

If your soil forms hard clods when it dries after a rain and standing water is slow to drain, Stevia plants probably won't be happy there. Raised growing beds can help the situation. Raised beds are great for improving drainage in heavy soils and will help prevent soil compaction.

Fig. 2-1: Raised growing beds. *Beds with cedar wood sides in the foreground and without sides in the background.*

Fertilization

Stevia is not a heavy feeder. Good compost is probably the best and only fertilizer needed. The slow release of nutrients from organic matter is the ideal delivery method for Stevia. Chemical fertilizers may be assimilated too fast, causing lush growth, lower in glycosides and more susceptible to diseases.

Excess nitrogen in particular can be a problem, especially with readily available chemical fertilizers. If you use a chemical fertilizer, it should pretty much have a balance of nitrogen, phosphorous, and potassium, or have more phosphorous and potassium than nitrogen.

A garden can benefit from a soil test done through your local University Extension Agency (U.S.) or a private testing lab. Home testing kits are available as well. In heavy clay soils, potassium is usually present at adequate levels. Sufficient nitrogen may be provided by dilute fish fertilizer, compost, composted manure, or a legume "green manure" crop.

Phosphorous may need attention. For organic gardens, phosphorous can be supplied by a dusting of rock phosphate or bone meal prior to digging or tilling in your compost. This will gradually break down and be available in the soil for years to come.

Transplanting

Green Manure

A "green manure" crop can improve soil texture and boost organic matter. It means growing some sort of crop and tilling or digging it in. Legumes such as beans or peas will add nitrogen. Cereal crops such as oats, wheat, or annual rye develop an extensive network of fine roots, improving soil texture. Peas and oats are a good cool weather combination. In areas with cold winters, oats die out so as not to become a weed problem the following year. Wait a few weeks between digging in the cover crop and planting your actual crop to allow time for decomposition.

Fig. 2-2: Young plant ready to transplant. *In 3-inch pot.*

Stevia seeds are so small and expensive that direct seeding in the final growing bed isn't advised. You'll want to obtain plants started from seeds or cuttings. Several mail order nurseries have perfected packaging that permits successful shipment of stevia plants. Check the appendix for a list of suppliers.

Some local greenhouses, nurseries, and farmer's markets are featuring Stevia plants as well. Ask around and see if you can find plants locally. You could also propagate plants yourself. Chapters 4 and 5 tell how to start your own transplants from seed or cuttings.

Location

If you have a choice of locations, Stevia prefers full or partial sun exposure. If your summers are very hot, afternoon shade will be beneficial. In fact, you may want to cover your plants with some type of shade fabric or other shading material in the hottest part of the summer and for new transplants (see figure 2-4).

If your summers are cool and cloudy, allow as much sun exposure as possible. Try to avoid locations prone to standing water. Raised beds will be helpful if such an area must be used.

Transplanting day

Try to transplant on a cloudy day or in the evening. Use a trowel to set the plants a little deeper than they were in the pot, spaced 12–14 inches (30–36 cm) apart. A bed 3 feet (or 1 meter) wide can hold two rows of plants. Gently firm the soil around each plant with your hands.

Fig. 2-3: Raised beds with Stevia plants. *These growing beds are 3 by 5 feet (about 1 by 1.5 meters) with 6 plants per bed.*

Avoid walking or kneeling on the bed itself. Water plants with a gentle soaking. Plants grow slowly at first and accelerate as the weather warms.

Timing for Transplanting

Timing for cold winter areas

In areas with cold winters, transplant at least two weeks after your last average frost date. In northern Missouri's USDA Hardiness Zone 5, for instance, the last frost date is around the first week of May. Find your own last average frost date online or ask at your local greenhouse, nursery, or University Extension Agency. Stevia plants dislike the cold soil and air of early spring. Harden plants off for about 4–6 six days before transplanting by placing outdoors in a protected area. Bring indoors at night if temperatures are forecast to dip below about 40° F. (4° Celsius).

Timing for frost-free areas or greenhouse

In a frost-free climate or a greenhouse without artificial light, your earliest possible transplanting date will be dictated by hours of daylight rather than outdoor temperatures. If plants are consistently exposed to less than about 12–13 hours of daylight per 24 hour period, they could go to seed early rather than producing maximum leaf yields. In the northern hemisphere (North America, Europe, etc.), you can generally count on enough daylight starting in early April. In the Southern hemisphere (South America, Australia, etc.), wait until early October.

Timing with artificial lighting

With artificial lighting such as a fluorescent shop light, you can provide 15 hours of light per day any time of the year, generally insuring vegetative growth. In that case, your transplanting date would not be constrained by natural day length (see chapter 3 about houseplants). Occasionally, some genotypes (genetic lines) may blossom even with longer day lengths. On young plants, remove blossoms until blossoming ceases and vegetative growth takes over.

Timing near the equator

Very close to the equator, you have about 12 hours of daylight every day of the year. In this case, plants will generally enter a blooming cycle whenever they reach sufficient maturity. You will get leaf growth—just slower than under long day conditions. Day length will not dictate outdoor transplanting time near the equator. Other factors like rainfall patterns might be important, however.

Plant Care

In the first few days after transplanting, protection from full direct sunshine will help plants adjust to their new home. If it is already hot and dry, mulch right away with straw, hay, shredded leaves, or grass clippings. Normally, wait until it gets consistently warm before placing organic mulches. In the U.S. Midwest, this would usually be June.

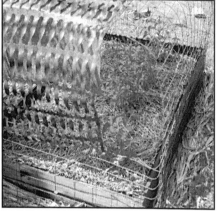

Fig. 2-4: Raised bed with shade cover. *Plastic snow fencing attached to frame made from wire fencing provides partial shade on a hot day.*

Growers in some areas have had good results with opaque plastic mulch or weed guard fabrics. They help with weed control and would be appropriate especially where summers are cool, as they tend to warm the soil.

With regular plastic mulch, rain can't get through, so a drip hose must be used. Install the drip hose before putting down the plastic. Weed guard fabrics are a special kind of mulch that will block weeds while allowing rainfall to penetrate from above. Place transplants through holes punched in plastic mulch or weed guard fabric.

Watering

When watering by hand, try to avoid getting leaves wet. It's a good idea to install a drip hose (also known as soaker hose) if you have too many plants to easily water by hand. Black rubber "weeping" hoses do an excellent job in garden-size plots.

In a bed with two rows, a single drip hose down the middle might be adequate, but two rows would be better. Run the drip hose up one side of the bed, make a U-turn, and back down the other side. (see

Fig. 2-5: Mulched plants with drip hose. *Straw mulch and recycled rubber "weeping" drip hose. Drip hose could be installed underneath mulch to reduce evaporative water loss a bit.*

figure 2-5). During dry spells, turn the hose on at a slow trickle for a few hours every 4–6 six days. Probe the ground with a trowel to see if your watering schedule is getting moisture about 6 inches (15 cm) deep.

A watering timer can be helpful with a drip hose. These battery operated devices go between the spigot and garden hose. They turn the water flow on and off at pre-determined times. Make sure the spigot is not open too far, as water flow must be low for most weeping drip hoses to work properly.

Pruning

Stevia stems are brittle and tend to break in the wind. Pruning stem tips to promote branching will help, and should be done anyway for maximum leaf yield.

When the main shoots are 8–12 inches (20–30 cm) in length, simply pinch or cut off 2–5 inches (5–13 cm) of the growing tips. This will force side branches to sprout where leaves join the stem, creating a bushy plant less prone to breakage (see figure 2-6).

When side branches reach 7–10 inches (18–25 cm) in length, prune their tips as well unless the growing season is more than about half over. Pruned leaves taste good eaten on the spot, especially combined with mint leaves. These leaves may also be dried or used fresh to make herb tea.

Fig. 2-6: Pruned stevia plant. *About 2 weeks after removing tips from main stems, this outdoor plant is producing nice side branches.*

Horizontal Stems

Sometimes, especially with seed-grown plants, a main stem will manage to lay down on the ground without breaking. The horizontal stem position sends a branching signal to the plant. Numerous vertical side branches sprout and grow vigorously without the usual tip pruning of the main stem. These shoots quickly grow straight up and produce a nice leaf yield (see figure 2-7).

Fig. 2-7: Horizontal stem with vertical side branches. *The main stem was lying on the ground and sent up vertical side shoots as long as 24 inches (61 cm).*

Plant Support

At very windy locations, plants may need support to minimize broken stems, whether it is main stems as in figure 2-8 or the side branches growing up from a stem laying on the ground as in figure 2-7.

A "corral" made with stakes around the perimeter of the bed and strings between may be adequate support. Wire fencing panels supported horizontally above the plants can provide support as well. Plants grow up through the wires. Metal T-posts or wooden stakes can support strings or fencing panels.

Fig. 2-8: Mature stevia plant. *These tall stems could be susceptible to breaking in high wind.*

Fencing panels can be self-supporting by forming them into an arch or hoop over the plants. The edges may need to be secured to stakes, bricks, concrete blocks, or timbers.

Pests and Diseases

Insect pests are seldom an issue for stevia outdoors. White-flies and aphids can be a problem with greenhouse production. Insecticidal soap sprays will usually deal with these soft-bodied pests. Insect predators such as ladybugs and lacewings are another option for controlling aphids.

Diseases are not usually severe for stevia, though bacterial and fungal diseases have been observed in some locations. Avoiding waterlogged soils and wet leaves will minimize diseases. When you see damage, remove that portion of the plant if it is isolated. Your local University extension agency or other plant professionals may be able to diagnosis nutrient deficiencies and diseases or they can send samples to a laboratory.

Perennial Production Outdoors

Plants grown as perennials should be mulched with 4–6 inches (10–15 cm) of straw or hay during the winter where winters temperatures tend to go below freezing at all. Mulch helps winter survival. Above-ground portions of plants usually do not survive if temperatures drop much below freezing, but plants may sprout back from the base as long as winter temperatures remain above about 25° F. (4° Celsius).

Plant roots will sometimes survive much colder temperatures with a deep mulch. During a Missouri winter (2005–2006), 3 out of 12 deeply mulched plants in a test plot survived temperatures as low as 10° F. (–12° Celsius). Plants were harvested in the fall of 2005, leaving behind stems about 3–6 inches (8–15 cm) in length. Before the first freeze, they were mulched with 8–12 inches (20–30 cm) of straw and leaves— enough to keep the ground from freezing. The mulch was held in place by plastic sheeting or snow fence material weighted with bricks. Mulch was removed after danger of frost in the spring. The 3 surviving plants eventually sprouted from the roots, but got off to a slow start and production was less than from new plants.

Chapter 3

HOUSEPLANTS

Stevia can be a challenging houseplant during the short days of winter because it wants to go to seed with short day lengths. Artificial lighting helps tremendously, however.

Plants can be held over from one season to the next and even produce leaves for use during the winter. Over-wintered plants can also be a source for taking cuttings in late winter or early spring.

With a large pot like the one pictured in figure 3-1, a stevia plant can be kept permanently potted for a few years, moved outside on the deck or patio when the weather allows.

Fig. 3-1: Large potted plant.
This plant is featured on the cover. The pot is about 10 inches (25 cm) in diameter.

Overwintering Outdoor Plants

In a cold-winter climate, plants can be dug up from your outdoor garden and kept alive indoors over the winter. At the final harvest, leave 3-5 inch (8-13 cm) stubs. The plants may then be dug right away or left to re-grow a little until frost threatens.

When digging, try to leave most of the roots intact. Most first year plants may be kept over winter in pots as small as 4 inches (10 cm) across and 8 inches (20 cm) deep (see figure 3-2). Older plants will need larger pots. Bury roots a little deeper than they were in the garden. Water gently to settle the soil.

Once the plants are a few years old, they may get too large for easy over-wintering. At that point you may want to start new plants from seed or cuttings.

Fig. 3-2: Newly dug plants.
Recently dug from the garden for over-wintering, these first year Stevia plants are starting to sprout new shoots. The pots are recycled and originally held raspberry plants. They are about 4 inches (10 cm) wide and 8 inches (20 cm) deep.

Watering Houseplants

Pour water in the dish or flat and let the soil absorb it from below. When using a pot that doesn't lend itself to bottom watering, you can water from above, but try not to get the leaves wet. Let the top of the soil dry out between waterings. Duration between waterings depends on pot size, temperature, and humidity. Smaller pots require more frequent waterings. When soil moisture is adequate, you should be able to poke your finger in a little and feel slightly moist soil. If the leaves begin to droop, plants may be too dry or too hot.

Potting up houseplants

"Potting up" means transferring a plant to a larger pot. Purchase potting soil or make your own (see sidebar). Young plants just started from seed or cuttings may be kept in small pots or cells for about 8-10 weeks, then transferred to larger pots. Plants older than about 2 years will need the largest pots, up to 10 inches (25 cm) in diameter (see figure 3-1). Pots should have drainage holes.

Bury plant roots a little deeper than they were in their old pot and water gently from above to settle the soil. Thereafter, it is best to water from below if possible.

Fertilizing Houseplants

Stevia requires little fertilization when grown in good potting soil. Plants permanently kept in pots will be more likely to need fertilizer. A few drops of commercial houseplant fertilizer, dilute fish fertilizer, or liquid seaweed in the water every few weeks or according to label directions will perk them up.

Fig. 3-3: Young houseplant. *This plant is about 4 months old and has been transplanted to a 5 inch (13 cm) diameter pot.*

Potting Soil

Just about any potting soil designed for houseplants will work for Stevia. A homemade recipe could include equal parts of the following ingredients, well mixed:

- compost
- black peat (or peat humus)
- sphagnum peat moss
- horticultural perlite

For long-duration use, add a dash of rock phosphate and greensand to reduce need for fertilization later. These ingredients are available at garden centers. In the case of compost, you can also make your own (see page 15), but remove large clumps and debris by sifting with a ½ inch (13 mm) screen.

Lighting for Houseplants

Artificial lighting is very beneficial for stevia plants during the short days of winter. Inexpensive fluorescent lights work well, producing wavelengths required by plants. A shop light with standard fluorescent bulbs is adequate, but special bulbs for plants are available as well.

With artificial lighting, plants can be kept alive and growing in a basement, garage, or spare room kept as cool as 55° F. (13° Celsius).

Fig. 3-4: Overwintering plants indoors. *These Stevia plants are thriving in a cool basement under fluorescent lighting.*

Keep the light on about 15 hours each day. This will usually keep plants in a vegetative state rather than going to seed.

Stevia plants can survive the winter with just light from windows, but the survival rate is likely to be lower. Stevia top growth will be rather poor during the winter, but don't be discouraged. After cutting back old winter growth, spring sunshine usually leads to healthy new growth as with the potted plant pictured in figure 3-5. New shoots will often sprout from below the soil surface.

Houseplants in the Spring

When spring arrives and days grow longer, plants may be placed outside to get some sun. Bring inside when temperatures are predicted to drop below about 40° F. (4° Celsius).

Starting about early April in the northern hemisphere or early October in the southern hemisphere, artificial lighting will no longer be needed to prevent blossoming in most cases. Daylight is usually sufficient at that point.

After danger of frost is over, plants may be transplanted to an outdoor garden if desired. It is probably best to start with new plants every 3–5 years, as old ones tend to eventually decline in vigor or outgrow their pots. Purchase new plants or start your own from cuttings or seeds.

Fig. 3-5: Potted plant in the spring.
This plant is featured on the cover. Winter growth has been harvested and new shoots are springing up, prompted by the long days of spring.

Chapter 4

PROPAGATION BY CUTTINGS

A stem cutting is a portion of plant stem that produces roots and shoots, forming a new plant! Stevia is a good candidate for this kind of propagation. Stevia cuttings root fairly easily in the winter with artificial light or during the long days of spring and summer. Here's what you'll need for this project:

- A mother plant from which to take cuttings
- Sharp knife or razor blade
- Growing medium: horticultural vermiculite, perlite or lightweight potting soil
- Pots or cell packs with drainage holes.
- Dish or tray for bottom watering
- Fluorescent shop light (or sunlight)
- Container with clear cover for humidity and warmth (if needed)

Making Cuttings

Choose a mother plant with enough growth to provide stems for cuttings. It may be a garden plant or a potted plant. Use a sharp knife or razor to make clean, slanting cuts. A long shoot can be sliced into smaller cuttings. Each cutting should be 3–5 inches (8–13 cm) in length. Remove larger leaves. Any small leaves growing in behind the larger ones may be left on the upper portion of

**Fig. 4-1:
Stem cutting.**
With large leaves removed.

the cutting. All leaves should be removed from the lower portion of the cutting (see figure 4-1).

Gently insert cuttings into the growing medium with the end that was closer to the base of the plant pointed down. The end that was further from the base should be pointed up. At least two leaf buds should remain above ground. Leaf buds are

Fig. 4-2: Newly planted cuttings.
A plastic cell pack with 6 cells.

at the axis where older leaves attach to the stem. Small leaves may be forming there already. This is the case in figures 4-1 and 4-2. Large leaves have been removed, leaving only the smaller secondary leaves or stem tips.

Caring for Cuttings

Use small pots or cell packs with holes in the bottom and water from below as needed to maintain a moist medium. If leaves begin to droop, the air is probably too dry. Periodic misting or a clear covering can help maintain humidity around the cuttings. The clear plastic "clamshell" boxes that hold lettuce or prepared pineapple from the grocery store work well for a small number of cuttings (see figure 5-2). They come complete with clear plastic lids, forming a "mini-greenhouse." Leave lid ajar to allow a little air flow. Don't let the temperature inside the "mini-greenhouse" exceed about 80° F. (27° Celsius). Remove cover completely when plants begin to grow.

Cuttings thrive with natural light when days are long. But a simple fluorescent shop light works even better. Leave the light on 24 hours per day for about the first week. Hang the light so the height can be adjusted to control temperature, especially when a "mini-greenhouse" is used. 70°–80° F. (21°–27° Celsius) is the optimum temperature range at first. After the first week, cooler temperatures are acceptable and the light should be left on about 15 hours per day.

After 3–4 weeks, successful cuttings will be growing and developing roots, possibly poking out from the drainage holes as in figure 4-3. At this point, transplant successful cuttings to larger pots with regular potting soil (see page 25 about potting soil). Allow to grow another 3–4 weeks before transplanting outdoors (or keep as potted plants if you prefer).

Fig. 4-3: Rooted cuttings.
At 4 weeks old, two of these cuttings show significant growth. You can also see roots growing out of drainage holes. These plants are ready for bigger pots and nearly ready for their first tip pruning.

When the longest shoot(s) reach about 3.5–4 inches (9–10 cm) in length, it's time for the first pruning to promote branching. Cut off 1-2 inches (2.5–5 cm) from the tip of the main shoot(s). There will usually be two dominant shoots, but sometimes just one—especially when the cutting was taken from a shoot tip rather than the middle of a stem.

Outdoor Propagation from Cuttings

Outdoors during the long days of spring, cuttings will sometimes root simply by inserting them into the ground near a drip hose where they will have constantly moist soil. Poke a hole in the ground with a small stick to help the cuttings go in more easily. These cuttings should be somewhat longer and inserted deeper into the ground than with potted cuttings. This will help prevent them from drying out if you forget to turn on the drip hose during a dry spell. Those cuttings that begin to grow noticeably after 3-4 weeks probably have new roots. They may be dug up and transplanted to their final location.

Chapter 5

PROPAGATION FROM SEED

Stevia is fairly easy to start from seed as long as the seeds are good. In the past, it was usually started from cuttings because good seeds were hard to find. In conducting research at Northwest Missouri State University, I found it is possible to produce high germination seeds. I also found that black or dark colored seeds tend to be more viable (link to Jeffrey's research at www.steviaseed.com).

Good Stevia seeds (generally over 70% germination), are now available. Sources are in the appendix.

Seeds not planted within a few weeks should be stored in an airtight glass jar such as a canning jar. For storage longer than about 6 months, it's best to put a desiccant in the jar with the seeds (see sidebar).

If you already have a favorite method for starting seeds indoors, it will probably

Fig. 5-1: Stevia seeds with penny. *Most seed companies remove pappus bristles, as with the seeds on the right in this photo.*

Seed Storage

Stevia seeds stored a long time like to be kept dry and cool. Place your packet of seeds in an airtight jar with a small amount of desiccant. Color changing beaded silica gel works well. These solid beads are treated to change color when saturated, at which point they can be dried and re-used (see appendix for sources).

Keep the jar in your refrigerator. Stored this way, good stevia seeds can remain viable for years. In our tests, seeds retained most of their germination ability after 7 years, while a batch of seeds stored at room temperature and humidity dropped from 90% to 75% germination in just 7 months.

work fine for starting stevia seeds. Just keep in mind that exposure to light helps germination slightly. Otherwise, requirements are similar to those for starting tomatoes from seed. Following is our favorite method for starting seeds indoors.

Shopping List for Seed Starting

- Nursery flat without drainage holes. Large plastic flats measure about 11 by 21 inches (28 by 53 cm) and 2.5 inches (6.35 cm) in height (figure 5-5). The larger plastic "clamshell" containers that hold greens from the grocery store work nicely as small flats (figure 5-2).

Fig. 5-2: Recycled clamshell flat. *This container originally held a pound of lettuce. As a "mini-greenhouse," it will hold up to 3 cell packs (6-packs).*

- Pots or cells-packs. 4-pack or 6-pack cell packs often come with nursery flats, or use small containers such as yogurt containers. Add drainage holes in the bottom.

- Clear cover. Nursery flats often come with molded plastic covers. Plastic wrap applied loosely will work in a pinch. The recycled "clamshell" containers mentioned above come with lids that work beautifully, forming a "mini-greenhouse." Just remove the label.

- Fluorescent light that can be hung for height adjustment. Special plant bulbs are available, but regular bulbs will do. Two full-size flats fit under a 4 foot (1.22 meter) long fluorescent shop light.

- Potting soil. Purchase potting soil or make your own (see page 25). Equal parts of peat moss (or peat humus), horticultural vermiculite, and compost will also work. Compost and peat should be sifted with a ¼ inch (6 mm) screen.

- Horticultural vermiculite for covering seeds.

- Seaweed fertilizer, dilute fish fertilizer, or another weak fertilizer. This is optional, but a good idea when there is no compost or fertilizer in the potting soil.

- Spray bottle or mister for misting the flat.

- Thermometer. A small dial-type model is ideal.

Directions for Seed Starting

Timing
In cold-winter climates, seedlings should be transplanted to the outdoor garden at least two weeks after your usual last frost date (we usually transplant about mid May here in Missouri—USDA zone 5). In frost-free climates, it's best to wait for long day lengths before transplanting to the outdoors (see "Timing for transplanting," pages 17–18).

Plants reach good transplanting size in about 8–10 weeks. Count back 8-10 weeks from your desired transplanting date to determine when to plant seeds.

Filling pots
If the potting soil is dry, moisten it slightly, mixing water in thoroughly. Fill cells or pots level full, without compaction of the potting soil. Place cells or pots in a flat or tray.

Seed selection
For best results, use only black or dark colored seeds. If you cut one in half, you'll see black seeds are usually solid and white inside. That's the healthy embryo.

Seed planting

Place 1–3 seeds on top of the soil in each cell or pot—more for old seeds with a lower germination rate. Seeds may be handled by pouring them out on a sheet of white paper. Pick up one seed at a time with the tip of a wet toothpick and transfer to the cell or pot.

Cover seeds about 1/8 inch (3–4 mm), preferably with fine horticultural vermiculite. A little potting soil may be used if you can't find horticultural vermiculite.

Spray gently with a spray bottle or mister. This will settle seeds and remove air pockets. Put a little water in the bottom of the flat as well. This will be absorbed from the bottom through the drainage holes. You shouldn't have to water again until plants are up and growing.

Fig. 5-3: Newly planted cell packs.
12 cells with thin layer of horticultural vermiculite covering seeds.

Lighting, humidity, and warmth

Place the clear cover on the flat to maintain warmth and humidity. Leave it slightly ajar to allow some air flow. Put a thermometer under the cover as well.

Place the flat under a fluorescent light left on 24 hours per day and hung so the height can be adjusted, such as with S-hooks and chains. Keep the air temperature between 75° and 80° F. (24°–27° Celsius) inside the enclosure by adjusting the height of the light. In most cases, the light will provide all the heat necessary.

In 7–14 days, you should begin to see tiny seedlings emerge. Remove the cover when more than half the pots or cells have seedlings showing. Seedlings could succumb to disease if the air remains humid too long. After removing the cover, continue to leave the light on all day and position it about 4–5 inches (10–13 cm) above plants.

When seedlings are old enough to tell which one in each pot or cell is strongest, cut the others off. At about three weeks from sowing, begin to turn the light off at night. Maintain about 15 hours of light each day. A timer is nice for this job.

Fig. 5-4: Young seedlings.
It's time to thin these seedlings to 1 per cell.

Fig. 5-5: Cell packs under fluorescent light.
Twelve 6-packs for a total of 72 cells. Two of these flats fit under a standard shop light hung above the plants. Several types of vegetable and herb seedlings are growing in this flat. The light should normally be kept about 4-5 inches above the tallest plants.

Watering

Water only from below. This avoids getting leaves wet. Pour about ¼ inch (6 mm) of water in the bottom of the flat for the pots to soak up. Wait 3–5 days before watering again unless the soil dries out sooner. The goal is to keep the soil moist, but not soggy. Put a few drops of seaweed fertilizer or other weak, low nitrogen fertilizer in the water starting around the third watering if the potting soil does not already have fertilizer or compost in it.

Pruning and transplanting

When seedlings reach about 5 inches (13 cm) tall, they should be pruned to promote branching. Simply cut off about 1-2 inches (2.5–5 cm) from the tip of the main shoot. This will also be your first leaf harvest!

At about 8–10 weeks from sowing, plants in small cells or pots should be transplanted to the outdoor garden or potted up to bigger pots. Pots 4–5 inches (10–13 cm) across are adequate for young plants, but larger pots allow for less frequent watering.

Harden plants off for four to six days before transplanting to the outdoor garden by placing them outside in a protected area during the day. Bring inside when temperatures are forecast to drop below about 40° F. (4° Celsius).

In our experience, Stevia leaves from seed-grown plants are often larger, but taste just like leaves from plants started by cuttings. Seed-grown plants tend to require more pruning or pinching to promote branching.

Fig. 5-6: Young Stevia plant from seed. *This plant has been growing outside in the garden for a few weeks.*

Fig. 5-7: Stevia seedlings in cell packs.

Chapter 6

HARVEST AND STORAGE

When it comes to harvesting, the obvious method is grazing in the Stevia patch! Just pinch off a leaf and enjoy. It's even better with a mint leaf. You can also make tea with fresh leaves. Use a tea ball or tea strainer just as you would make any herb tea.

Leaves can be harvested any time, but you'll get the highest leaf yield just as plants start blooming, usually late summer or fall. When the first blossom buds form (see figure 6-1) or you see the first blossoms, go ahead and harvest. When growing Stevia as a perennial, you will want to leave about 6 inches (15 cm) of the plant to allow for re-growth.

Fig. 6-1: Sprig with blossom buds. *This stem is about to produce blossoms at the tip, so it has probably reached maximum leaf yield.*

Drying Leaves

Cut whole stems with a scissors or pruner and tie into small bundles with a rubber band. Use a bent paper clip to hang bundles upside down in a well ventilated location, preferably out of direct sun. Stretch strings across the ceiling for more hanging space.

Leaves will be crispy in a few days. When they are completely dry, strip leaves by hand and discard stems (they don't taste as good). Soft stem tips may be kept along with leaves.

Another drying method is to strip leaves from stems while still fresh and spread on a food-safe wire rack or tray out of direct sun or in a food dehydrator on low heat (under 110° F. or 43° Celsius). When completely dry, leaves are ready for making tea, further processing (see chapter 7) or storage.

Storing Dried Leaves

Dried Stevia leaves may be stored at room temperature in an airtight jar out of direct sunlight. They keep well this way for years.

Fig. 6-2: Dried leaves on stems. *Leaves ready to be stripped from stems and stored.*

Fig. 6-3: Drying Stevia leaves on a rack. *Fresh leaves on the left and dried on the right. The cookie sheet catches leaves that fall through.*

Chapter 7

PROCESSING STEVIA LEAVES

Whole Dried Stevia Leaves are ready for making herbal tea alone or in combination with other herbs. Mint or chamomile are great with Stevia. We think most herbal teas are better with the addition of Stevia.

Dried Stevia Leaves may be purchased if you run out of home-grown. Check the appendix for sources. Following are ways to make further use of homegrown or purchased Dried Stevia Leaves. Recipes in chapter 9 make use of Stevia Leaf Water Extract and Green Stevia Powder.

Stevia Leaf Water Extract yields about ½ cup extract

Alcohol or glycerin extracts are available for purchase, but we prefer this water extract. It keeps about 2 weeks in the refrigerator and works well for many beverages and some other recipes.

- ½ cup *Dried Stevia Leaves*, packed in the measuring cup
- 1 cup water

Bring water to a simmer in a small saucepan. Small bubbles should come to the surface. Stir in Dried Stevia Leaves, turn off heat, and cover the pan. Steep 40 minutes. Store in a very clean glass jar. Cover with a lid and refrigerate. Use within 2 weeks.

Green Stevia Powder
yields about 1/3 cup powder

The most versatile Stevia product from homegrown plants, you'll find recipes using Green Stevia Powder in this book and more in "Stevia Sweet Recipes: Sugar-Free—Naturally!" by Jeffrey Goettemoeller. Green Stevia Powder is also available for purchase at some natural food stores or online (see appendix).

- 2 cups *Dried Stevia Leaves*, packed down in the measuring cup

Place dried stevia leaves in a blender bowl and cover while blending on high speed for 30 seconds. Leave bowl covered a few minutes, allowing dust to settle inside. Remove cover and stir with a rubber or plastic spatula, then put cover back on and blend another 30 seconds at high speed.

Alternatively, this first step may be done with a flour sifter or mortar and pestle, in the absence of electricity or an electric blender. With a flour sifter, put in a handful of leaves at a time, cover, and turn the handle until most leaf material has disintegrated and fallen through the screen. Throw out any remaining leaf veins or debris. When using a mortar and pestle, thoroughly grind a few leaves at a time.

Regardless of the grinding method, the powder may be used in recipes at this point if desired, or sift through a tea strainer to remove larger particles still remaining. This removes some tough leaf veins that resist dissolving and don't taste as good.

For long term storage, put the powder in a glass jar with a tight lid and keep in a dark place. It stores at least 2 years this way without loss of flavor. Short term, Green Stevia Powder may be stored in a recloseable plastic bag kept in a dark location. In general, 3–4 teaspoons of Green Stevia Powder replaces a cup of refined sugar.

Chapter 8

STEVIA IN THE KITCHEN

S tevia is available for purchase in different forms, including the following:

- Dried Stevia Leaves (whole dried leaves)
- Green Stevia Powder (powdered leaves)
- Liquid Stevia Extracts (alcohol, glycerin, or water-based)
- Stevia Extract Powder (extract of glycosides)

Here we are primarily concerned with *Dried Stevia Leaves, Green Stevia Powder,* and *Stevia Leaf Water Extract* since these can be made in your kitchen from homegrown or purchased Stevia leaves (see chapter 7) and then used in the recipes in chapter 9.

Unlike aspartame, Stevia is heat stable. It works in a variety of dishes when the recipe is properly designed. Dry Stevia products also have a long shelf life.

Certain issues present a challenge when cooking with Stevia. Very little is required due to its tremendous sweetness. Bulk normally provided by sugar must instead be supplied by other dry ingredients. Also, some way must be found to distribute Stevia evenly through the other ingredients.

The taste of Stevia can also be a challenge, especially with Green Stevia Powder and Liquid Stevia Extracts. Stevia is sweet, but with its own unique flavor, just as honey and sorghum have their own flavors. This is not a problem if the ingredients are adjusted and selected so they interact harmoniously with Stevia. In fact, Green Stevia Powder can act as a flavor enhancer at times, bringing out flavors of other ingredients.

Dried Stevia Leaves

Whole dried leaves may be purchased (see appendix) or grow your own! Either way, they make a sweet and delicious herbal tea. Stevia leaves enhance the flavor of most other tea herbs when mixed together. Dried Stevia Leaves are also the raw ingredient for making other stevia products. Dried Stevia Leaves may be stored at room temperature in an airtight jar out of the sunlight. They will keep well this way for many years.

Fig. 8-1: Dried Stevia leaves.
Dried leaves store well for years in a glass jar with a tight lid.

Green Stevia Powder

Green Stevia Powder consists of Dried Stevia Leaves that have been finely ground. It can be made in the kitchen from homegrown or purchased leaves (see chapter 7). Green Stevia Powder contains the full range of nutrients found in Stevia. It does present some challenges, with its green color and stronger taste. It doesn't work in just any recipe, but works well in recipes found in chapter 9.

Store Green Stevia Powder in a glass jar with a tight lid and keep in a dark place at room temperature. It stores at least 2 years this way without loss of quality. A recloseable plastic bag kept in a dark location will be adequate for short-term storage.

Conversion rate: A good rule of thumb is to use 3–4 teaspoons of Green Stevia Powder in place of 1 cup refined cane sugar. But the conversion rate varies greatly depending on the recipe.

Liquid Stevia Extracts

Liquid extracts are convenient for sweetening beverages and some other dishes. Most liquid extracts on the market have an alcohol or glycerin base to extend shelf life. Stevia Leaf Water Extract can be used in some of the recipes in chapter 9 and may be made in your own kitchen from dried leaves by following the directions in chapter seven (page 43). Stevia Leaf Water Extract can be kept in the refrigerator for about a week.

Stevia Extract Powder

Most Stevia recipe books, including Jeffrey's *Stevia Sweet Recipes: Sugar-Free—Naturally!*, call for pure Stevia Extract Powder, which must be purchased. The extraction process is beyond what you would want to tackle at home. This white or off-white powder is an extract of the sweet glycosides in the Stevia plant. Because of their unique structure, these glycosides don't contribute calories to the diet. The main glycosides are stevioside and rebaudioside A. Stevia Extract Powder contains 80–95% glycosides. The term "stevioside" is used by some authors as a collective term for all the glycosides found in the Stevia plant.

We prefer a pure Stevia product, with no maltodextrin or other fillers. These fillers may not be tolerated by those who must avoid easily metabolized carbohydrates, and the pure

Stevia Extract Powder is almost always a better buy in terms of sweetening power for your money. Additionally, some fillers dissolve poorly.

Conversion rate: We find that one teaspoon of Stevia Extract Powder has roughly the sweetening power of one cup refined cane sugar, though the conversion rate varies greatly depending on the ingredients with which it is combined.

Chapter 9

RECIPES

These 35 recipes use *Dried Stevia Leaves* (for tea), *Green Stevia Powder, or Stevia Leaf Water Extract*—products that can be made at home from homegrown or purchased stevia leaves! Just follow the directions in Chapter 7.

Data for nutritional information are approximations and some nutrient information might not be available for user-added ingredients. Nutritional information was provided by the *Recipe Analyzer* software from Ohio Distinctive Software, Inc. and *The Whole Foods Companion* by Dianne Onstad, published by Chelsea Green.

Metric Conversion Chart

The recipes in this book were developed using U.S. measures. The following chart gives approximate metric equivalents for your convenience.

U.S. Volume	Metric Volume
1/16 teaspoon	.31 mL
1/8 teaspoon	.62 mL
1/4 teaspoon	1.25 mL
1/2 teaspoon	2.5 mL
1 teaspoon	5 mL
1 tablespoon	15 mL
1/4 cup	34 mL
1/3 cup	46 mL
1/2 cup	69 mL
2/3 cup	92 mL
3/4 cup	102 mL
1 cup	137 mL
2 cups	274 mL
1 ½ cups	206 mL
1/2 gallon	3.79 liters

U.S. Weight	Metric Weight
1 ounce	28 grams
4 ounces	113 grams
1/2 pound (8 ounces)	227 grams
12 ounces	340 grams
15 ounces	425 grams
1 pound (16 ounces)	454 grams

U.S. Length	Metric Length
1 inch	2.54 centimeters
9 inches	23 centimeters
10 inches	25 centimeters
13 inches	33 centimeters

Simple Stevia Tea

yields 1 cup

Stevia is our favorite tea herb by far, with a delicious flavor and soothing to the tummy.

- 1 cup water
- Approximately 1 teaspoon *Dried Stevia Leaves*, slightly crushed (a few leaves)

Pour the water into a saucepan. Place Dried Stevia Leaves in a tea ball or loose directly into the water. Bring to a simmer and leave on burner for 3–5 minutes. Remove tea ball or strain with a tea strainer to remove loose leaves. Serve when tea cools sufficiently.

Variation: Other dried or fresh tea herb leaves such as mint may be combined with stevia leaves as desired.

Hot Tea, Green

yields 1 cup

- 1 cup water
- 1 teaspoon *Dried Stevia Leaves*, slightly crushed (a few leaves)
- 1 green tea bag

Bring water to just under boiling. Little bubbles should come to the top. Stir in Dried Stevia Leaves and add the green tea bag. Cover and steep 5 minutes. Strain and serve.

Variation: Black tea is made in the same way using one tea bag.

Blueberry Grape Syrup

yields 1 pint syrup

Great topping for pancakes or ice cream!

- 1 cup grape juice
- 2 cups blueberries, fresh or frozen
- 1 tablespoon cornstarch or arrowroot powder
- 1 tablespoon *Green Stevia Powder*
- 2 tablespoons lemon juice

Place grape juice, blueberries, cornstarch or arrowroot, and stevia in the blender bowl. Process until smooth. Pour into a saucepan and cook over medium heat, stirring constantly. When syrup has thickened, reduce heat to simmer and cook for 3 minutes longer. Remove from heat and stir in lemon juice. Use right away or refrigerate. May be used cold from the refrigerator or gently reheat.

Puffy Oven Pancake

yields 6 servings

- 2 tablespoons butter
- 3 extra large eggs
- ½ cup whole grain wheat flour
- ½ cup milk
- ¼ teaspoon *Green Stevia Powder*
- ¼ teaspoon salt or sea salt
- ¼ teaspoon vanilla extract or maple flavoring

Place butter in a 10 inch oven-proof skillet or cake pan. Place in 400° F. (204° Celsius) oven for 3–5 minutes or until butter melts.

In a bowl, beat eggs until combined. Add flour, milk, Green Stevia Powder, vanilla or maple flavoring, and salt. Beat until smooth. Immediately pour into the hot skillet or pan. Bake about 25 minutes or until puffed and well browned. Serve with your favorite fruit topping, sauce, or *Blueberry Grape Syrup* (page 52).

Variations:
- *Rice flour may be substituted for wheat flour.*
- *Soymilk or rice beverage may be substituted for dairy milk.*

NUTRITION INFORMATION PER SERVING
Calories – 122
Carbohydrates – 8 gm
Protein – 5 gm
Fat – 7 gm
Sodium – 184 mg
Fiber – 1 gm
Calcium – 43 mg
Vitamin A – 370 IU
Vitamin C – 0 mg

Spiced Oat, Nut, & Fruit Granola yields about 7 cups

- ¼ cup sunflower seeds
- ¼ cup wheat flour
- 2 cups rolled oats
- 1 cup coarsely chopped walnuts or pecans
- 6 tablespoons unsalted butter
- 1 tablespoon *Green Stevia Powder*
- 1 ½ teaspoons cinnamon
- ¼ teaspoon salt
- 3 tablespoons water
- 2 eggs
- 2 tablespoons honey
- 3 tablespoons unsweetened coconut
- 1 cup raisins or other dried fruit

Preheat oven to 325° F. (163° Celsius).

In a medium mixing bowl, combine sunflower seeds, flour, oats, and nuts. Set aside.

Melt butter in a medium saucepan. Cool to lukewarm and stir in Green Stevia Powder, cinnamon, salt, water, and eggs. Stir this mixture into the sunflower seed mixture. Press into a buttered 9 x 13 inch baking pan.

Bake 15 minutes. Remove from oven and stir. Cook another 15 minutes and stir again. Bake a final 15 minutes (a total of 45 minutes in all).

Remove from oven and drizzle with honey. Sprinkle surface with coconut and raisins. Stir to combine. Cool and store in a covered container in the refrigerator. Also freezes well for longer-term storage.

Variation: Seven teaspoons of Stevia Leaf Water Extract can be used in place of the Green Stevia Powder. In this case, omit the plain water from this granola recipe.

> Unsalted Butter: It's best to use unsalted butter in recipes because the amount of salt added to salted butter can vary.

Gluten-Free Granola

- ¼ cup sunflower seeds
- ¼ cup rice flour
- 2 cups quinoa *flakes*, uncooked
- 1 cup coarsely chopped walnuts or pecans
- 6 tablespoons unsalted butter
- 1 tablespoon *Green Stevia Powder*
- 1 ½ teaspoons cinnamon
- ¼ teaspoon salt or to taste
- 3 tablespoons water
- 2 eggs
- 2 tablespoons honey
- 3 tablespoons unsweetened coconut
- 1 cup raisins or other dried fruit

Preheat oven to 325° F. (163° Celsius).

In a medium mixing bowl combine sunflower seeds, rice flour, quinoa flakes, and nuts. Set aside.

Melt butter in a medium saucepan. Cool to lukewarm and stir in Green Stevia Powder, cinnamon, salt, water, and eggs. Stir this mixture into the sunflower seed mixture. Press into a buttered 9 x 13 inch baking pan.

Bake 15 minutes. Remove from oven and turn granola in sections with a wide spatula. Cook another 15 minutes and turn again. Bake a final 15 minutes (a total of 45 minutes).

Remove from oven and drizzle with honey. Sprinkle surface with coconut and raisins. Stir gently to combine. Cool and store in a covered container in the refrigerator. Also freezes well for longer-term storage.

Variation: Seven teaspoons of Stevia Leaf Water Extract can be used in place of the Green Stevia Powder. In this case, omit the plain water from this granola recipe.

> Quinoa Flakes: Quinoa is a gluten-free grain. In some recipes, quinoa flakes can be used in place of rolled oats or part of the flour.

Breakfast Oatmeal

yields 3 servings

- 2 ¼ cups water
- 1 teaspoon *Green Stevia Powder* OR 1 tablespoon *Stevia Leaf Water Extract*
- 1 cup old fashioned rolled oats
- milk or yogurt (optional)

Bring water to a boil in a saucepan. Stir together Stevia and rolled oats and add to water. Cook for 5 minutes over medium heat while stirring occasionally. Remove from heat, cover and set aside for 3 minutes before serving. Top with milk or yogurt.

Cinnamon Apple Oatmeal

yields 3 servings

- 1 ¼ cups apple juice
- 1 cup water
- dash cinnamon
- ½ teaspoon *Green Stevia Powder*
- 1 cup old fashioned rolled oats
- milk or yogurt (optional)

Place juice, water, cinnamon, and Green Stevia Powder in a saucepan. Bring to a boil. Add oats. Cook for 5 minutes over medium heat while stirring occasionally. Remove from heat, cover and set aside for 3 minutes before serving. Top with milk or yogurt.

Breakfast Sausage

yields 6 patties

- 1 teaspoon olive oil plus more for frying
- 2 teaspoons light soy sauce or similar condiment
- 2 teaspoons rubbed sage
- 1/8 teaspoon allspice
- ¼ teaspoon *Green Stevia Powder*
- Pinch of crushed red pepper flakes or ground turmeric
- 1/8 teaspoon nutmeg
- ½ teaspoon crushed dried basil
- ½ teaspoon ground coriander seed (optional)
- Salt and pepper to taste
- 1 pound ground beef
- ½ cup grated apple—any variety (about ½ of an apple)

Measure seasonings (olive oil through salt and pepper if used) into a mixing bowl and stir to mix. Add ground beef and apple and combine. Cover and refrigerate 2 hours or overnight.

Pour oil into skillet, form patties and cook slowly over low heat. Use pan drippings to season another dish such as scrambled eggs.

Variation: Ground chicken, turkey, or bison can be used with this recipe. In this case, increase olive oil to 2 teaspoons.

Vanilla Nut 'Ice Cream'

yields 4 servings

- 3 ½ bananas, peeled
- ½ cup apple juice
- ¼ teaspoon *Green Stevia Powder*
- 1 ½ teaspoons vanilla
- 1/3 cup plain low-fat yogurt
- 2 tablespoons natural peanut butter

At least a day before making this recipe, break the bananas into chunks, drop in a plastic bag, seal, and freeze.

Place the remaining ingredients in a blender container. Add a few of the frozen banana chunks and blend on low speed, gradually increasing speed to a higher setting. Add remaining banana a few pieces at a time. If mixture becomes too thick to process, add a bit more apple juice. Serve immediately.

NUTRITION INFORMATION PER SERVING
Calories – 171
Carbohydrates – 30 gm
Protein – 4 gm
Fat – 5 gm
Sodium – 55 mg
Fiber – 3 gm
Calcium – 49 mg
Vitamin A – 112 IU
Vitamin C – 16 mg

Orange Stevia Soda

yields 6 ¼ cups soda

- 4 ½ cups seltzer water (carbonated water)
- 12 ounces (1 ½ cups) frozen orange juice concentrate
- ¼ cup S*tevia Leaf Water Extract*

Allow frozen orange juice concentrate to melt until completely or mostly liquid. Combine all ingredients in a pitcher or ½ gallon jar. Stir briefly. Best enjoyed immediately. Carbonation will disperse over time. Cover tightly and refrigerate any leftovers.

Chocolate Milk Shake

yields 2 servings

- 2 bananas, peeled
- 1½ cups milk (soymilk or rice beverage may be substituted)
- 2 teaspoons cocoa powder
- 2 teaspoons *Green Stevia Powder* or 7 teaspoons *Stevia Leaf Water Extract*
- ½ teaspoon vanilla extract

At least a day before making this recipe, break the bananas into chunks, drop in a plastic bag, seal, and freeze.

Place half the banana chunks and remaining ingredients in a blender bowl. Process on medium, then increase speed to a higher setting. Gradually add remaining banana pieces and process until smooth. Serve immediately.

Peach Smoothie

yields 3 servings

- 2–3 bananas, peeled
- 2 cups frozen peach slices, unsweetened
- 1 teaspoon *Green Stevia Powder* OR 1 tablespoon *Stevia Leaf Water Extract*
- 1/16 teaspoon cinnamon
- 2/3 cup water

Place all ingredients in the blender bowl in the order listed and process until smooth. Be sure to cover the blender bowl while processing. Start at low speed and work up to higher speeds. Serve immediately.

Strawberry Soup

yields 4 ½ cups soup

- 3 cups fresh or frozen strawberries, hulled
- ¾ cup sugarfree white grape juice
- ¾ cup plain lowfat yogurt
- ¾ teaspoon *Green Stevia Powder* or 2 tablespoons *Stevia Leaf Water Extract*

Puree strawberries and juice in a blender. Be sure to cover the blender bowl while processing. Stir in remaining ingredients and chill at least 2 hours in the refrigerator. Stir and serve.

Variation: Also delicious with a sugarfree cherry juice blend in place of grape juice.

Strawberry Smoothie

- 2–3 bananas, peeled
- 1 tablespoon *Stevia Leaf Water Extract*
- 2 cups frozen strawberries
- 1/8 teaspoon vanilla extract
- 2/3 cup water
- ¼ cup plain yogurt (optional)

Break bananas into chunks and place in the blender bowl. Add the Stevia Leaf Water Extract, 1 cup of the strawberries, the vanilla extract, and water. Briefly process at low speed and gradually switch to higher speeds with blender bowl covered. Add remaining strawberries a few at a time and process until smooth. If desired, add the yogurt for extra creaminess. Serve.

Variation: This smoothie can be made with fresh strawberries. In this case, freeze bananas in chunks ahead of time. Process the strawberries, water, and vanilla extract first. Then gradually add the banana chunks and process until smooth.

Chocolate Chip Cookies

yields about 26 cookies

- ¼ cup butter, softened
- 2 teaspoons *Green Stevia Powder*
- 1 large egg
- 3 tablespoons prune juice
- 1 teaspoon vanilla extract
- ¾ cup flour, white or wheat
- ¼ teaspoon baking soda
- ¼ teaspoon salt
- ½ cup chocolate chips
- ½ cup coarsely chopped walnuts

Preheat oven to 325° F. (163° Celsius)

Using a whisk or wooden spoon, cream together butter and Green Stevia Powder. Add the egg, prune juice, and vanilla extract and combine well. Sift together flour, baking soda, and salt. Stir into the butter mixture and then add chips and nuts, mixing just to combine.

Drop cookies on lightly oiled cookie sheets. Bake 10 or 11 minutes. Remove to a cooling rack.

Variation: For gluten-free cookies, substitute ¾ cup gluten-free flour in place of white or wheat flour and add ½ teaspoon Xanthan gum. Mix and bake as above.

> Xanthan Gum is a powder sometimes used to replace gluten in baked recipes such as breads and cookies. Available in many natural food stores.
>
> Gluten is a type of protein found in many grains. Gluten-free ingredients are available for those with a gluten intolerance.

Lime Pie

- 1 recipe *Lemon Chiffon Topping* (page 67)
- 2 teaspoons *Green Stevia Powder*
- 3 tablespoons cornstarch
- 1 cup water
- 1 cup orange juice
- 1 extra large egg
- 3 oz. cream cheese
- 1/8 teaspoon lemon extract
- ¼ cup fresh lime juice
- 1 pie shell, 9 inch, baked

Prepare Lemon Chiffon Topping and refrigerate.

Combine Green Stevia Powder, corn starch, water, orange juice, and egg in a saucepan. Cook over medium heat until thickened. Reduce heat to low and cook a minute longer. Remove from heat. Stir in cream cheese, lemon extract, and lime juice. Cool to room temperature. Spoon into pie crust and refrigerate 2–3 hours. Briefly stir Lemon Chiffon Topping and pile on top of the filling. Chill overnight.

Rhubarb Strawberry Pie

yields a 10 inch pie

- Pastry for a 10 inch, 2 crust pie
- ¾ cup whole wheat pastry flour (any whole grain flour may be substituted)
- 2 tablespoons *Green Stevia Powder*
- 3 cups fresh rhubarb ribs, cut in pieces
- 3 cups fresh strawberries, hulled and sliced
- 2 tablespoons butter

Fit bottom pastry into a pie dish.

Stir together flour and Green Stevia Powder in a large mixing bowl. Add rhubarb and strawberries and stir to coat well. Turn into the prepared pastry. Dot with butter.

Moisten the outer rim of the lower crust with water. Place upper crust on top and crimp edges to seal. Slit upper crust to let steam escape. Bake 30 minutes at 400° F. (205° Celsius). Reduce heat to 350° F. (177° Celsius) and bake an additional 30 minutes. Cover with foil the last 15 minutes to prevent over-browning. Cool on a rack. Cover and refrigerate overnight. Also good served at room temperature.

NUTRITION INFORMATION PER SERVING
Calories – 121
Carbohydrates – 15 gm
Protein – 2 gm
Fat – 5 gm
Sodium – 84 mg
Fiber – 3 gm
Calcium – 51 mg
Vitamin A – 310 IU
Vitamin C – 28 mg

Blueberry Pie

- 1 pie shell, 9 inch, baked

Ingredients for blueberry filling:
- 1 ½ cups unsweetened white grape juice
- 4 tablespoons cornstarch
- 2 ¼ teaspoons *Green Stevia Powder*
- 3 cups unsweetened frozen blueberries
- ½ teaspoon vanilla extract

Ingredients for cream cheese layer:
- 4 ounces cream cheese (half of an 8 ounce package)
- 1/3 cup plain yogurt
- ½ teaspoon vanilla extract
- 2 tablespoons unsweetened white grape juice
- ¼ teaspoon *Green Stevia Powder*

Combine 1½ cups white grape juice, cornstarch, 2¼ teaspoons Green Stevia Powder, and blueberries in a saucepan. Cook and stir over medium heat until mixture thickens. Add vanilla extract and stir in. Set pan in ice water to cool.

In a small, deep mixing bowl, beat together cream cheese, yogurt, vanilla extract, 2 tablespoons white grape juice, and ¼ teaspoon Green Stevia Powder. Spread this mixture in the baked pie shell. Top with blueberry filling. Chill at least 3 hours before serving.

Variations:
- *Any berry juice can be used in place of white grape juice.*
- *¼ cup Stevia Leaf Water Extract may be used in place of the Green Stevia Powder in the blueberry filling (also reduce grape juice to 1 ¼ cups).*
- *2 teaspoons Stevia Leaf Water Extract may be used in place of the Green Stevia Powder in the cream cheese layer (also reduce grape juice to 1 tablespoon).*

Carob Silk Pie

yields 8 servings

Try serving with Chiffon Topping (p. 67) or Whipped Cream

- 1 1/3 cups carob chips
- 2 tablespoons vegetable oil
- 1 package (12 ounces) firm tofu
- 1 teaspoon *Green Stevia Powder*
- 1 teaspoon vanilla extract
- 1/8 teaspoon orange extract, optional
- 2/3 cup plain yogurt
- 1 pie shell, 9 inch, baked

Melt carob chips with oil in a heavy saucepan over low heat. Place the remaining ingredients in a blender bowl. Add carob chip mixture and process until smooth. Pour into the pie shell. Chill.

Coconut Whipped Cream

yields 2 ½ cups topping

Delicious on shortcake, pie, or other desserts.

- ½ cup light coconut milk
- 1 cup whipping cream
- 1 teaspoon *Green Stevia powder*
- 1 teaspoon vanilla extract
- ¼ teaspoon almond extract (optional)

Chill a small mixing bowl and the beaters for your electric mixer. Open the coconut milk and measure out ½ cup of the thick part of the milk from the can. Reserve remaining milk for another use.

Add the rest of the ingredients. Whip until medium peaks remain when the beaters are lifted (overbeating will result in lumps). Serve immediately or reserve in refrigerator a short time.

Variation: Other flavorings and spices may be used.

Lemon Chiffon Topping

- 2/3 cup water
- 1 teaspoon unflavored gelatin
- ½ cup nonfat dry milk
- 1 teaspoon vanilla extract
- 1/8 to ¼ teaspoon lemon extract
- 1 teaspoon *Green Stevia powder*
- dash salt
- 4 tablespoons vegetable oil

Pour water into a small saucepan. Shake gelatin on top and set aside to soften 5 minutes. Dissolve over low heat, stirring as needed. Remove from heat and stir in dry milk, vanilla and lemon extracts, Green Stevia Powder, and salt. Transfer to a mixing bowl. Chill until partially set. Beat for 4 minutes. Add oil and gradually beat in. Topping will be very light. Refrigerate. Stores well in the refrigerator.

Variation: For Vanilla Chiffon Topping, omit lemon extract and increase vanilla extract to 1 ¼ teaspoons.

Baked Custard

- 3 extra large eggs
- 1 ½ cups milk
- 1 ¼ teaspoon *Green Stevia Powder*
- 1 ½ teaspoon vanilla extract
- 1/8 teaspoon cinnamon

Whisk eggs. Add remaining ingredients and whisk again. Cover and chill one hour to blend flavors. Whisk briefly. Pour into 5 custard dishes. Place dishes in a flat baking pan. Pour very hot water around the dishes to a depth of one inch. Bake at 325° F. (163° Celsius) for about 50 minutes or until a knife inserted near center comes out clean. Refrigerate. Serve chilled.

Variation: Soymilk or rice beverage may be substituted for the dairy milk.

NUTRITION INFORMATION PER SERVING
Calories 94
Carbohydrates 4 gm
Protein 6 gm
Fat 5 gm
Sodium 81 mg
Fiber 0 gm
Calcium 110 mg
Vitamin A 444 IU
Vitamin C 0 mg

Pumpkin Custard

yields 8 servings of ½ cup each

- 4 eggs, lightly beaten
- 1 can (14 ounces) light coconut milk
- 3 ½ to 4 teaspoons *Green Stevia Powder*
- ½ teaspoon cinnamon
- ¼ teaspoon nutmeg
- 1/8 teaspoon salt, or to taste
- 1 ½ teaspoon vanilla extract
- 2 cups cooked pumpkin or 1 can (15 ounces) *plain* pumpkin (*not* pre-spiced pumpkin pie filling).
- Plain yogurt for topping (optional)

Preheat oven to 325° F. (163° Celsius)

Using a medium mixing bowl or mixing pitcher, whisk ingredients together in the order listed, adding pumpkin last. Pour ½ cup custard into each 6 ounce custard cup. Place cups in a 9 x 13 inch baking pan. Carefully pour hot water around cups to a depth of about 1 ½ inches. Bake until a knife inserted in custard comes out clean, about 50 to 55 minutes. May be eaten warm or chilled.

Grape Kiwi Salad

yields 4 servings

- 2/3 cup plain lowfat yogurt
- ¼ teaspoon *Green Stevia Powder*
- ¼ to ½ teaspoon dry lemon peel
- 3 tablespoons orange juice
- 1 ½ cups washed and halved grapes
- 3 kiwifruit, peeled and cubed
- torn lettuce or mixed greens
- 3 fresh Stevia leaves, shredded (optional)

Whisk together first four ingredients for dressing. Chill.

Stir fruits together. Arrange lettuce on serving plates. Spoon fruit onto lettuce. Drizzle with dressing. Garnish with fresh stevia. Serve immediately.

Variation: One cubed apple can be added to the fruit.

Pineapple Berry Gelatin

yields 8 servings

- 4 cups sugar-free berry juice (Sold as combination of juices)
- 2 envelopes unflavored gelatin
- 1 teaspoon *Green Stevia Powder* OR 1 tablespoon *Stevia Leaf Water Extract*
- 1/8 teaspoon lemon extract (optional)
- 2 cups pineapple tidbits or chunks (one 20 oz. can, drained)

Pour one cup of the juice into a saucepan. Sprinkle gelatin over surface and set aside to soften for 5 minutes. Place pan over low heat and stir to dissolve gelatin. Remove from heat and stir in remaining juice, Stevia, lemon extract, and fruit. Turn into a serving bowl. Refrigerate. When partially gelled, stir to distribute fruit. Chill.

Variations: Sliced canned fruit can be substituted for pineapple. Almond or orange extract can be substituted for lemon extract.

Sweet 'n Spicy Meatballs

- 1 teaspoon prepared mustard
- 2 teaspoons reduced-sodium soy sauce
- ¼ cup unsweetened applesauce
- 1 teaspoon *Green Stevia Powder*
- 3 tablespoons water
- 1 teaspoon minced dry onion
- ¼ teaspoon ground ginger
- 1 pound lean ground turkey
- 1 ½ teaspoons minced dry onion
- ¼ teaspoon poultry seasoning, optional
- salt to taste, optional
- butter or oil to sauté
- chopped fresh parsley
- cooked brown rice, still hot

In a small bowl whisk together mustard, soy sauce, applesauce, Green Stevia Powder, water, 1 teaspoon minced dry onion, and ginger. Set aside.

With a fork mix turkey with 1½ teaspoons minced dry onion, poultry seasoning, and salt. Heat butter in a medium skillet. Form meat into 20 meatballs and brown in skillet over medium heat. Reduce heat to low and pour mustard mixture over meatballs. Cook about 20 minutes or until meatballs are thoroughly cooked and no longer pink inside. Spoon onto a platter of hot rice. Sprinkle with parsley.

Savory Spaghetti Sauce

yields about 6.5 cups

Rich, homemade flavor, but easy to make! Tweak with your family's favorite spices, but the secret is the green stevia powder. The stevia enhances all the flavors. Add Special Garlic Toast (page 73) and a salad for a complete family dinner!

- 1 pound ground beef
- 1 medium onion
- 2 cloves garlic
- 2 teaspoons Italian seasoning
- ½ teaspoon *Salt-Free Herbal Seasoning* (page 75)
- 4 teaspoons basil, dried
- ½ teaspoon *Green Stevia Powder*
- 1 can tomato paste (6 ounces)
- 2 cans plain* diced tomatoes (15 ounces per can)
- 1 cup water
- Salt and pepper to taste
- 1 can mushrooms or ½ pound fresh mushrooms (optional)
- ½ cup green bell peppers, chopped

Put ground beef in large pot or pan on medium high heat. Break up large pieces and stir occasionally until somewhat brown all over. You may want to drain off grease if there is much excess. Add onions and garlic. Continue to stir occasionally for 2–3 minutes longer. Add the rest of the ingredients and simmer on low heat for about 20 minutes. Serve over cooked pasta, rice, squash, or green beans.

Variation: Dried Stevia Leaves may be substituted for the Green Stevia Powder in this recipe. Crumble about 6 leaves in your fingers as you drop them into the sauce. Stir and wait 3-5 minutes. Then taste the sauce. Add more Dried Stevia Leaves if desired.

Pre-spiced diced tomatoes may be used instead, but lower the amount of spices you add to the sauce.

Special Garlic Toast

Green Stevia Powder enhances flavor, allowing you to use less salt on this classic favorite!

- Bread (we like the heavy, sprouted grain bread)
- butter
- sea salt
- garlic powder
- *Green Stevia Powder*

To make this as easily and fresh as possible, try this short-cut: Toast the bread in an ordinary toaster. Butter immediately and sprinkle on salt and garlic powder. Lightly dust the toast with a pinch of Green Stevia Powder. You do not need to completely cover the toast with any of the ingredients—especially the Green Stevia Powder. Experiment with the amounts, but remember that with stevia you will not need as much salt.

Herb Dumplings for Stew

- Vegetable or chicken stew to serve 8
- 2 cups whole grain flour, wheat or gluten-free
- 2 ½ teaspoons baking powder
- 1/8 teaspoon *Green Stevia Powder*
- 1 teaspoon salt, or sea salt
- 2 extra large eggs
- ½ cup milk
- 2 tablespoons vegetable oil
- 1 tablespoon fresh chopped parsley or ½ teaspoon dry parsley
- ½ teaspoon *Salt-Free Herbal Seasoning* (page 75)

Have stew cooked and simmering in a Dutch oven on the stovetop.

Stir together flour, baking powder, Green Stevia Powder, and salt. Set aside.

Combine eggs, milk, vegetable oil, parsley, and Salt-Free Herbal Seasoning. Mix well. Add to flour mixture and stir just to combine.

Drop dumplings by spoonfuls into stew and cook 12–14 minutes on low heat. Remove a dumpling and cut open to see if it is done. Serve hot with the stew.

Salt-Free Herbal Seasoning   yields about 9 teaspoons
Great on salads, sandwiches, soups, pasta, fish, & meat dishes.

- 2 teaspoons dried crushed basil
- ¼ teaspoon ground coriander seeds
- 3 teaspoons onion powder
- ¼ teaspoon *Green Stevia Powder*
- 1 teaspoon garlic powder
- ½ teaspoon dried thyme
- 2 teaspoons dried parsley flakes
- ¼ teaspoon turmeric, optional

Combine ingredients in a shaker-top container that can be tightly closed. Seasoning may settle slightly, so shake briefly before using.

Creamy Herb Salad Dressing   yields about ¾ cup
Try this dressing on mixed vegetables or a pasta salad!

- 1/3 cup mayonnaise
- 1/3 cup plain yogurt
- ¼ teaspoon *Green Stevia Powder*
- 2 teaspoons fresh lemon juice or ¼ teaspoon lemon zest
- ¼ teaspoon dried parsley flakes
- Salt to taste (optional)
- ¼ teaspoon *Salt-Free Herbal Seasoning* (recipe above)

Stir all ingredients together in a small wide-mouth jar. Cover with a lid. Refrigerate.

Variation: For use on a fruit salad, omit the Salt-Free Herbal Seasoning.

> Zest is the flavorful outer part of citrus fruit peels. Remove with a fine grater. Use only the colored layer.

Sunflower Oat Rolls

- ¼ cup vegetable oil
- 1 1/8 cup water
- 1 extra large egg
- 2 ½ cups bread flour
- 1 cup whole grain flour
- ¼ cup toasted wheat germ
- ¼ cup oat bran
- ¼ cup sunflower seeds
- 1 tablespoon poppy seeds (optional)
- 1 teaspoon *Green Stevia Powder*
- 1 teaspoon salt
- 2 ½ teaspoon active dry yeast

Add all ingredients to bread machine in the order given by the manufacturer's direction for the machine. Activate the whole wheat bread dough cycle. At the end of the first rising cycle, take dough out and divide into 20 pieces. Shape into rolls. Place 2 inches apart on a greased baking sheet. Cover with a clean kitchen towel and put in warm place. Let rise until double in size, about 45 minutes. Remove towel and bake in a 375° F. (191° Celsius) oven for 12 minutes. Cool on wire racks. Can be sliced most of the way through and frozen for later use.

Pumpkin Muffins   yields 12 small muffins

Freeze a batch for an easy snack. Thaws in just a few minutes. Great with butter or jam on top.

Dry ingredients:
- 1 ½ cups white rice flour (or wheat flour)
- 2 teaspoons baking powder
- ¼ teaspoon sea salt
- 1 ½ teaspoons cinnamon
- ½ teaspoon nutmeg
- ½ teaspoon allspice or cardamom
- ½ teaspoon *Green Stevia Powder*

Wet ingredients:
- ¼ cup vegetable oil
- ¾ cup cooked and mashed or blended pumpkin (or canned pumpkin)
- ½ teaspoon almond or vanilla extract

Preheat oven to 400° F. (204° Celsius) and lightly grease a 12 tin muffin pan.

Mix dry ingredients in a large mixing bowl. In another bowl, stir together the wet ingredients.

Add wet ingredients to the dry ingredients. Stir briefly until all batter is moistened. It is acceptable to have a few lumps in the batter. Divide among the 12 muffin tins. Bake in preheated oven for 18–20 minutes or until slightly browned on top.

Variation: Add 1/3 cup raisins or chopped nuts after adding dry ingredients.

Rice Tomato Soup

yields 4 servings (1 cup each)

- 2 cups rice milk
- 2 cups tomato juice or 1 can (14.5 ounces) diced tomatoes with their juice
- 1 clove garlic, sliced
- 3 teaspoons minced dry onion
- 2 ribs celery, sliced
- ¼ teaspoon *Green Stevia Powder*
- 3 tablespoons butter
- 2 or 3 tablespoons rice flour

Heat rice milk in a saucepan until near a simmer.

Measure remaining ingredients into blender bowl. Process until smooth. Add to the hot milk. Bring soup back to a simmer while stirring. Simmer 5 minutes. Serve as is or with one of the following garnishes:

- Yogurt or sour cream
- Mayonnaise
- Snipped chives
- Salt-Free Herbal Seasoning (page 75)

Appendix

STEVIA SOURCES & RESOURCES

The following is not an exhaustive list, but we present these contacts for your information. We have not dealt with all of these companies, so inclusion here does not necessarily represent an endorsement.

Company

Items Available

Seedman.com
1917 Summerlin Bayou Rd.; Vancleave MS 39565
www.seedman.com

Stevia Seeds
Green Stevia Powder
Stevia Extract Powder

Prairie Oak Publishing
221 S. Saunders St.; Maryville MO 64468
(660) 528-0768 www.prairieoakpublishing.com

Stevia Seeds and books,
wholesale & retail

Morgan County Seeds
18761 Kelsay Rd.; Barnett MO 65011
(573) 378-2655 www.morgancountyseeds.com

Stevia Seeds

Cal Stevia
13739 Old Westside Rd.; Grenada CA 96038
(530) 436-2610 www.cal-stevia.com

Live Stevia Plants, Seeds
Green Stevia Powder
Stevia Extract Powder

Heirloom Acres LLC
PO BOX 194; New Bloomfield MO 65063
(573) 491-3001 www.heirloomacresseeds.com

Stevia Seeds

Suede Hills Organic Farm
BC Canada www.steviasweetsuccess.com

Green Stevia Powder

Company	Items Available
Ayer Market and Greenhouse Rt. 2 BOX 302; Bluford IL 62814 (618) 732-8558	Live Stevia Plants, Seeds Green Stevia Powder Stevia Extract Powder
Pinetree Garden Seeds PO BOX 300; New Gloucester ME 04260 www.superseeds.com	Stevia Seeds
J. W. Jung Seed Company 335 S. High St.; Randolph, WI 53957-0001 (800) 247-5864 www.jungseed.com	Live Stevia Plants Stevia Seeds
Seed Savers Exchange 3094 N Winn Rd; Decorah IA 52101 www.seedsavers.org	Stevia Seeds
Fountain of Youth–Gojiseed.com 2478 State Hwy 92; Winterset, IA 50273 (515) 462-2352 www.fountainofyouth-gojiseed.com	Stevia Seeds
Nichols Garden Nursery 1190 Old Salem Road NE; Albany OR 97321-4580 (800) 422-3985 www.nicholsgardennursery.com	Live Stevia Plants, Seeds Green Stevia Powder Stevia Extract Powder
Emperors Herbologist (904) 538-3838; www.emperorsherbologist.com	Green Stevia Powder Stevia Extract Powder
Herbal Advantage Inc. 131 Bobwhite Rd Rogersville MO 65742 (800) 753-9199 www.herbaladvantage.com	Live Stevia Plants Whole Dried Leaves Green Stevia Powder Stevia Extract Powder
Johnny's Selected Seeds 955 Benton Ave; Winslow ME 04901 (877) 564-6697 www.johnnyseeds.com	Stevia Seeds
Richters Herbs 357 Hwy 47; Goodwood ON L0C 1A0 Canada www.Richters.com	Live Stevia Plants Stevia Seeds Stevia Extract Powder
The Gourmet Gardener Florida www.gourmetgardener.com	Live Stevia Plants

Company	Items Available
Mountain Rose Herbs (800) 879-3337; www.mountainroseherbs.com	Stevia Seeds Green Stevia Powder
Stevia Canada / JG Group Burlington ON Canada; +1 905-634-8976 www.SteviaCanada.com; retail, wholesale, & bulk	Stevia Seeds Green Stevia Powder Stevia Extract Powder
Horizon Herbs PO Box 69; Williams OR 97544 www.horizonherbs.com	Stevia Seeds Live Stevia Plants
One Green World 28696 South Cramer Rd.; Molalla OR 97038 (877) 353-4028 www.onegreenworld.com	Live Stevia Plants
Crimson Sage Nursery PO BOX 83; Orleans CA 95556 www.crimson-sage.com	Live Stevia Plants
Garden Medicinals (434) 964-9113 www.gardenmedicinals.com	Silica Gel for seed storage
Southern Exposure Seed Exchange P.O. Box 460; Mineral, VA 23117 (540) 894-9480 www.southernexposure.com	Silica Gel for seed storage
Bountiful Gardens 18001 Shafer Ranch Rd; Willits CA 95490 (707) 459-6410 www.bountifulgardens.org	Stevia Seeds
Abundant Life Seeds PO BOX 279; Cottage Grove OR 97424-0010 (541) 767-9606 www.abundantlifeseeds.com	Stevia Seeds
Berlin Seeds 5335 County Rd 77; Millersburg OH 44654-9104 (330) 893-2091	Stevia seeds
Fedco Seeds PO Box 520; Waterville ME 04903 (207) 873-7333 www.fedcoseeds.com	Stevia Seeds

Resources for Additional Information

www.GrowingStevia.com (web site for *Growing & Using Stevia*)
Sign up for Jeffrey's free "Stevia Grower" E-Newsletter.
Download free pdf color slide show based on this book or the version
for commercial growers.

Stevia Sweet Recipes: Sugar-Free—Naturally!
by Jeffrey Goettemoeller • Square One Publishers
Recipes using mostly white *Stevia Extract Powder.* Available at
health food stores or these web sites:
www.stevia-recipes.com (includes free sample recipes)
www.squareonepublishers.com (wholesale & retail)

Growing Stevia for Market: Farm, Garden, and Nursery Cultivation of the Sweet Herb, Stevia rebaudiana.
by Jeffrey Goettemoeller • Prairie Oak Publishing
www.prairieoakpublishing.com

www.omafra.gov.on.ca/english/crops/facts/stevia.htm
Canadian government site on large scale Stevia cultivation

http://www.ksre.ksu.edu/ksherbs/stevia.htm
Results of Kansas State University commercial scale trials

Glossary

aphids—Soft-bodied, sap-sucking insects from 1–5 mm long. Sometimes infest young stevia leaves and stem tips. Usually not a serious problem outdoors. More often, aphids are a problem indoors or in greenhouses. Controlled by insecticidal soap or insect predators such as ladybugs or lacewings.

cell pack—Container for starting plants—usually small plastic pots or "cells" attached in a group. Common size is a 6-pack. Twelve 6-packs fit in a standard nursery flat. Nursery flats with cell packs are widely available and are ideal for starting large numbers of stevia or other bedding plants.

compost—Decomposed organic matter used as a soil amendment or growing medium. Sifted compost is often part of potting soil or seed starting mixes. Mixed into garden soil, improves soil structure and fertility. In most soils, compost is the only fertilization necessary for successful stevia production.

cutting—A section of plant stem used for asexual propagation. Stevia cuttings produce roots easily in a coarse growing medium.

dehydrator—Appliance with shelves or trays designed to dry food using low heat and circulating air.

direct seeding—Planting seeds directly in the ground outdoors. Not recommended for stevia because of small size and high cost of seeds.

drip hose—Hose for drip irrigation. Water weeps or drips slowly from emitters or tiny holes. Minimizes water use and wetting of plant leaves.

fish fertilizer—Fish-derived liquid or powder designed to provide nutrients to plants. Useful for stevia grown in low fertility soils when used in a more dilute solution than usual.

genus—A taxonomic category consisting of a group of plant species with similar characteristics. Within the *Stevia* genus, only the *rebaudiana* species contains large amounts of sweet glycosides.

germination—Emergence from a period of dormancy. Seed germination is the beginning of a growth cycle for plants like stevia.

gluten—A type of protein found in many grains. Gluten-free ingredients are available for those with gluten intolerance.

glycemic index—A measure of how fast a food causes a rise in blood glucose levels when consumed. Stevia leaf is considered low-glycemic, causing very little surge in blood glucose levels.

glycosides—A group of molecules in which the sugar part is bound to another part. Certain glycosides, stevioside and rebaudioside A being the most prominent, are responsible for the sweet taste of stevia. Rebaudioside A is considered to have the best quality of taste. Some authors use the term "stevioside" to mean all the glycosides in the stevia plant collectively.

green manure—Plants being grown for soil improvement.

greensand—A slow-release natural fertilizer formed in marine deposits. Supplies mainly potassium (potash) and many other trace minerals. It can be used in potting soil, as a garden soil conditioner, or as a top dressing.

Green Stevia Powder—Powdered dry stevia leaf. Made at home from dry leaves in a blender or with a mortar and pestle. Useful in some types of recipes.

insecticidal soap—Special soap designed to control certain pests such as aphids by a direct spray application.

last frost date—The average date of the last frost in spring. Stevia should not be outdoors without protection until a couple weeks after last frost date. Find your last frost date online or at your library or university extension agency.

loam—Soil consisting of sand, silt, and clay, usually with a lower proportion of clay. Ideal for many plants including stevia.

mother plant—Plant from which material is taken for propagating new plants.

mulch—Material placed on soil surface, usually to hold in moisture. Organic mulches such a straw, leaves, or grass clippings also keep the soil cooler, provide food for earthworms, and gradually enhance soil fertility.

nursery flat—A shallow container for holding young plants. Can be fitted with a clear dome for seed starting. The most common U.S. size is about 11 inches (28 cm) wide and 21 inches (53 cm) long.

organic matter—Soil organic matter is plant and animal material that has decayed. Vital for optimum soil structure and fertility. Can be supplied by mulching with organic materials or incorporating compost into the soil.

overwintering—Surviving through the winter season. In cold climates, Stevia usually needs to be brought indoors or otherwise protected from freezing temperatures over the winter. Artificial lighting helps as well.

perennial plant—Plant that normally lives more than two growing seasons. Stevia is a tender perennial, meaning it generally cannot survive outdoors where temperatures drop below freezing.

perlite—Type of volcanic glass. Horticultural perlite has been expanded and is light in weight. It has the appearance of white beads. It adds air spaces to potting and seed starting mixes and is a good medium for rooting cuttings.

plant propagation—The process of reproducing plants. Stevia is usually propagated by stem cuttings or seed.

potting soil—Medium for growing plants in containers. Should have proper balance of air space, water holding capacity, and necessary nutrients.

pruning—Removing a portion of a plant. Stevia stem tips should be removed every few weeks during the early part of the growth cycle. This promotes beneficial branching.

quinoa flakes—Quinoa is a gluten-free grain. In the form of flakes, quinoa can be used in place of rolled oats or part of the flour in some recipes.

raised bed—Low mound of soil, sometimes surrounded by wood, concrete, plastic, brick, or some other edging to contain the soil. Good for growing stevia in areas where soil drains poorly or is heavy (high in clay content).

rock phosphate—Rock with a high proportion of phosphate minerals. Phosphate is one of the macro-nutrients needed by plants and may be supplied by fertilizers derived from rock phosphate.

short day plant—Plant that blossoms only under short day conditions. *Stevia rebaudiana* falls under this category. It generally produces blossoms only with enough hours of darkness in every 24 hour period. In Missouri, this usually happens in late September. The long days of summer at high latitudes tend to suppress blossoming and encourage leaf production.

silica gel—Porous form of silica that acts as a desiccant (drying agent). Available as solid beads that change color when saturated. May be placed in a sealed jar with stevia seeds for long term storage. Can be dried and re-used.

simmering—Cooking technique. Liquid is kept just below boiling point. Done by bringing to a boil, then lowering heat until just a few bubbles are visible.

standing water—Water left on the surface of the ground after a rain. An area where water remains for a long time after a rain may be too waterlogged for optimum stevia production. A raised bed may help in such a situation.

steeping—Soaking something in a liquid. Steeping stevia leaves is part of the process for making stevia tea and Stevia Leaf Water Extract.

stem rot—Fungal disease of plant stems and leaves. Made worse by high humidity and cool temperatures.

Stevia—Genus name for a large group of plants and shrubs native to South and Central America. More commonly, the term is used for a particular species, *rebaudiana*, having a significant quantity of sweet glycosides.

Stevia Extract Powder—White or off-white powder consisting mainly of one or more of the glycosides from the *Stevia rebaudiana* plant.

Stevia Leaf Water Extract—Greenish liquid produced by steeping dried stevia leaves in hot water.

stevioside—Most prominent glycoside in *Stevia rebaudiana*. Some authors use this term when referring to all the glycosides found in stevia collectively.

sun exposure—Expression of how much direct sunlight strikes a plant. In most places, stevia thrives with full sun or with afternoon shade. During the summer in hot climates, additional shade may be needed and can be provided by shade cloth or other material attached to some kind of frame.

tea ball—Usually a hollow metal ball with holes. Make stevia tea by immersion in hot water with leaves inside.

tea strainer—Basket-like sieve with a handle. Make stevia tea by immersion in hot water with leaves inside.

temperate climates—The climates predominating between the tropics and the polar circles or in higher altitudes of some tropical regions.

tender perennial—A plant that generally survives more than two growing seasons, but only where temperatures remain mostly above freezing all year. Stevia is a tender perennial that can be treated as an annual (replanted every growing season) in colder climates.

transplant—Young plant meant to be moved to a new growing location or the act of moving a plant to a new growing medium.

University Extension Agency—Educates public on consumer issues, horticulture, and other topics in many states of the U.S.

USDA Hardiness Zone—Geographic zones based on climatic conditions. First established by the U.S. Department of Agriculture.

vermiculite—Natural mineral with a high cation exchange capacity. Horticultural vermiculite has been expanded and is light in weight. Useful for potting and seed starting mixes and covering stevia seeds for germination.

viable—For seeds, this means having the capacity for germination under favorable conditions.

whiteflies—Tiny sap-sucking insects. Congregate mostly on the underside of leaves. Sometimes infest Stevia, especially indoors. Control methods include insecticidal soap and predatory insects such as lacewings.

General Index

Recipe Index

Author Online

www.prairieoakpublishing.com
or
www.growingstevia.com

Sign up for Jeffrey's free "Stevia Grower" E-Newsletter. Download free pdf color slide show based on this book.

More Books from Prairie Oak Publishing

Growing Stevia for Market: Farm, Garden, and Nursery Cultivation of the Sweet Herb, Stevia rebaudiana. Author Jeffrey Goettemoeller. ISBN 978-0-9786293-5-9.

Sustainable Ethanol: Biofuels, Biorefineries, Cellulosic Biomass, Flex-Fuel Vehicles, and Sustainable Farming forEnergy Independence. Authors Jeffrey Goettemoeller and Adrian Goettemoeller. ISBN 978-0-9786293-0-4.

Organic Container Gardening: Grow Pesticide-Free Fruits & Vegetables in Small Spaces. Author Barbara Barker. ISBN 978-0-9786293-6-6.

Made in the USA
Lexington, KY
19 April 2013